GABRIEL'S
MESSAGES

GABRIEL'S MESSAGES

Cyndi Smith

RAVENSOUND
PUBLISHING

Author email: cyndimkjb@yahoo.com

Ravensound Publishing
Brisbane, QLD, Australia

Cover Illustration: Lane Heise
Typesetting: David Tensen

Messages from Gabriel / Cyndi Smith

ISBN 979-8-218-13697-0

DEDICATION

To humanity,

*I pray for your inner peace, your true
understanding of God's love for you,
your knowledge of the magnificent
beings you truly are, and for you to be
filled with pure joy and grace.*

With abundant love,

Archangel Gabriel

PREFACE

Angels and guides have talked to me throughout my life. I have always been able to communicate with them easily. For most of my life I have followed their guidance and advice. I have always felt watched over and protected. As a young child I soon realized that not everyone had the abilities I have. As a psychic medium I can feel the energies of places and understand that what a person says is not always what is truly in their heart. Once I understood that I was "different" in some ways, I was told by my guides and Angels to keep these gifts to myself until I was older and could understand them and use them to help myself and others too.

I was blessed to be born into a wonderful family. My parents were warm, caring and loving people. I couldn't have picked better parents. I have 2 brothers and 1 sister and they are not only my siblings they are close precious friends. I couldn't imagine life without them. After saying all that I am not sure my parents would've known what to do with me had they known about my gifts.

As a child of 3 or 4 I could astral travel at night with ease. I still remember the spinning sensation that happens when your soul is released from your body. I would travel out into space or just to my Nana's house at the shore. Travel was fun and all I had to do was think about where I wanted to go and I was there. It is still fun to do, but I can't release at will, like I used to.

When I was 13, I had a Near Death Experience. I was cutting the hedges at our house and I accidentally cut the cord to the clippers. I realized I was going to die as the electrical current ran through my body. I saw my life and felt the consequences of my actions both good and bad. Then I found myself in a hole surrounded by the greenest grass and looking at this beautiful blue sky, it was Heaven, and I saw other souls there too. Then everything changed and there was just this magnificent loving light. I knew it was God. He filled me with love, He actually poured it into me. I will never forget that feeling. Then He said "Cyndi, turn it off with your left hand." I was scared and knew if I touched it with my left hand it would get stuck like my right hand was. So I didn't move, but God did and He turned off the clippers. I was not hurt or burned, just scared. Later that day our neighbor brought the cord to our house, it was only cut about half way through. He asked how I was able to turn it off. As I looked at my parents and our neighbor I said "He turned it off for me." They never asked who

He was. They just assumed I had had a bad scare and let it go.

When I went to college at 18, I explored spirituality through books and psychics. I read all I could on NDE and finally understood what had happened to me. I realized I wasn't alone, that lots of people had similar experiences like me. Books became my teachers and as I learned and read, much of it felt right, like I had known all this before and was just remembering it again.

My gifts grew as I became more comfortable with them. I could "read" people easily and knew things about them that they didn't express. I have always been able to feel energy in places both good and bad. Learning about past lives made so much sense to me. I finally could look at hints about myself and remember some of the lives I had lived. Understanding about past lives helps me see why I carry feelings about certain places and things.

Later I worked as a Kindergarten teacher in a small private school, with other teachers who became my friends. I would receive messages from Spirit and pass them along to the teachers. This gave me the opportunity to practice with them and thus have validation for my abilities. I can "hear" the other side and have always been able to with ease, but now I was using it to help others, which I enjoyed. It was during this time that I also became aware that I was a medium and could communicate with those who had passed over. I was ready to open the door to do readings for people.

As I learned about past lives and the more knowledge I gained in the spiritual realm the more it "fit into place" for me. I know I have had these gifts before in other lives and have remembered many of the lives I have lived. It has been an ongoing process shared with friends and family of like mind. I continue to grow and learn everyday. I am so grateful for my loving family and friends who have supported, loved and cared for me throughout my life. I am eternally grateful for the divine guidance I have been given over my lifetimes. I would not be where I am without the help and support of the guides and Angels who have patiently worked with me.

INTRODUCTION

On April 26, 2020, just a month after the pandemic started, Archangel Gabriel came to me and said that he wanted to show me the future. I agreed and was immediately transported ahead in time, about 25 years.

After this fantastic journey I quickly wrote all that I had seen and learned from this remarkable trip. Gabriel explained that he wanted me to share this view of the future with the world so others would get excited and not be caught up in the current fear and panic of the pandemic. "The sooner people believe this is possible the faster this will become reality" he said. He wants everyone to release their fear and work toward this magnificent future.

I talked to my friends at the Center for Contemporary Mysticism. I have been a part of this group since its conception back in 2013. Patricia Pearce said she would do an interview and post it on our website. The Center has done in person monthly meetings for years with a variety of speakers and topics all spiritually based. Since the pandemic the Center had no choice but to do Zoom meetings only.

It wasn't until late fall that I agreed to post Gabriel's messages on my Facebook page. I am a rather private person, so it took some time for me to be comfortable with posting these. Gabriel told me he had additional messages he wanted people to read and know. My brother Paul's computer skills and my sister Sue's proofreading helped me post the the first Gabriel message in November of 2020. He had quickly started downloading another message to me so I posted that one in December of 2020. I soon realized he had a great deal he wanted to share and so his messages became monthly postings.

In January of 2022, Gabriel asked me to make a blog and put all of his messages on it. Again, with the help of my brother Paul, we started a blog where all his messages can be seen. In March of 2022, Gabriel hinted again he had more for me to do and in May he told me he wanted his messages to be made into a book.

Little did I know when I started this two years ago I would be creating a book. I have complete faith and trust in Gabriel, and I am eternally grateful for his trust in me. I am excited and honored to have this opportunity to share his messages with you.

ACKNOWLEDGEMENTS

First I want to thank my husband Bob. He has always supported and believed in me. His love, trust and care have never wavered. I love him and I am so grateful for all he has done for me.

I want to thank my children Karoline, Jeff and Bethany, you carry the best parts of Dad and me and we are so proud of the loving, caring people you have become. We love you.

To my friends and family I am so blessed to have you in my life. Thank you for all your love and support. You have enriched my life with your trust, help, friendship and love. What wonderful gifts you each are, you have added so much to my life.

To Lane, my dearest friend, thanks for sharing this life with me. I couldn't imagine doing this journey without you. You know me better than anyone.

To all of my CCM friends, you have given me a group of like minded friends to share my life with and I am grateful. Thank you for all you do.

To Archangel Gabriel, thank you for your trust and belief in me. You helped me to grow and I will be forever grateful.

ABOUT ARCHANGEL GABRIEL

The word Archangel comes from the Greek. An Archangel is a divine angel with a leading position within the group. There are 7 Archangels. Angels carry out God's desires for all creatures everywhere. Archangel Gabriel is known as the "Messenger of God." He helps God by delivering His messages. Gabriel was the angel who brought the news of Jesus' birth to Mary.

For me Gabriel is a friend, a very trusted friend. He asked if I would be willing to get his messages out, I said I would. Once he started downloading messages month after month to me we fell into a rhythm and it became a deeper and more personal connection for me.

As the holidays approached I would ask him for advice on where to find a certain item that I was shopping for, he always knew where to find it. Shopping with him was fun and he was never wrong. I have become familiar with his voice and can easily open for advice or help with a situation.

As my trust grew he would show me places and things so as I wrote his messages I had a better understanding of what he was speaking about. An example of this is love, love is visible to those of the higher realms as light, but I was shown how it looks, and how it travels throughout the universe connecting all planets, stars and other celestial bodies with iridescent threads of pulsating light. It is a beautiful web of light which feeds everything throughout the universe. This is God's love which feeds everything everywhere.

Gabriel's reason for connecting to me at this time is to help those in fear to realize how much power we all have and how loved we all are. Fear is the enemy of change and we are in the middle of a great transformation. We have the power to live in a utopian world if we just believe it is possible to do. Our own fear is what is holding us back.

Gabriel and other angels and guides have come to many other people just like me. I am not the only one to be tapped on the shoulder and asked to help get the message out. Lorna Byrne did a YouTube message in August of 2022, about the future of the planet, mankind and the changes that are taking place. Gabriel has spoken of these same outcomes for our Earth to me. Different words, same message. We are always being helped and guided, but especially now.

I feel very honored to be asked to help Gabriel get these messages out into the world.

TABLE OF CONTENTS

MESSAGE #1
MY TRIP WITH
GABRIEL

For those of you who don't know me, my name is Cyndi Smith, I am a psychic medium. I have had most of my gifts since birth. Angels and Guides have talked and guided me throughout my life. At the beginning of 2020 Archangel Gabriel came to me and told me that he had some messages he wanted me to get out into the world. He asked if I would help him. I agreed. I will begin today to share some of his messages.

Back on June 28th, of this year, I did a podcast for the Center for Contemporary Mysticism. I invite anyone who is interested to go to their website and check it out. It will have more details of this first encounter and messages from Gabriel. Their website is www.contemporarymysticism.org.

Gabriel's first real message to me was on April 26, 2020. He took me into the future where

I could see and feel my surroundings. It was a world full of peace, less stress and relaxed, a place we will want to live. What follows is what I saw.

Today Gabriel showed me what the future of our world will look like. In 10 years we will see great changes, in 25 years we will see a completely changed world. Fossil fuels will no longer be used, everything will be battery powered or run by some other renewable energy. Homes, cars, boats, airplanes, businesses all will be run with renewable energy. I saw large container ships all run by large batteries, no pollution went into the sea or air. There will be a worldwide involvement with healthcare, food, resources and economics. Most, but not all countries, will wish to be a part of this coalition. Our governments will work closely on many issues and decisions will be made for the good of the world.

It will be a very clean world, we will not permit pollution of any kind. More green space will be added or created, especially in cities. I saw large parks and lots of people enjoying the outdoor spaces. People will mostly work from home, but the technology will give us the tools to go to meetings in any part of the world. Bi-location will be a tool we can use and do with ease. We will attend meetings and school in this manner. Colleges will be able to use the world as their classroom through holograms. Trips can be virtual too. We will be able to go anywhere and experience every aspect of a place without leaving home. Our homes will be hubs of technology connecting us to the world. Technology will be a part of our lives but not running our lives. The home I saw was run with advanced technology, which will give us the opportunities to connect with many people. We will have gardens, and yards and will care for and use our outside spaces all the time. We work with technology, but we will not be run by it.

Life will be more relaxed, peaceful and spiritual. There will be pockets of people who will not wish this way of life, that will be each person's choice. We will pay a food tax which will send food to all corners of the world and help wipe out hunger.

The world will make universal decisions about many issues. We will still have individual rights and countries will still be separate and have their own laws but in many areas we will work as one, for the good of all. Many old ways will end in order for a new one to begin. Systems must break down so new ideas can emerge. We will learn to work together.

Medicine will be universal, you will be able to see any doctor in any part of the world. Surgeries will be performed in sacred spaces. Once the surgery is done you will be able to go home and doctors and nurses will be able to check in on you at your home. New jobs will emerge as needs create them.

Nature will be honored and she will set the rules. We will care for the Earth and keep her clean. Earth mirrors our fears or love. She shows it in the weather throughout the world. As our vibrations grow and we transition into higher levels she will also transition into higher levels. This will allow her weather patterns to calm and storms to be less severe.

We will still gather in groups and enjoy each other's company. We will not run and hurry but walk with ease.

As I was brought back from this amazing view of our future, I felt hopeful and excited for what is to come. I asked why is there a spread of 10 to 25 years? Gabriel said. "That the sooner people see this as their reality and start to believe that this is all possible the sooner it will happen." Our feelings, wants and desires determine our future. The more people believe in this future the faster it will manifest.

Right now we are going through difficult times of destruction. The old must be torn down in order for the new to be built. There will be more people sick, homeless and out of work. It will be a very dark time full of fear. Many can help by being healers. We need healers in the medical fields, but we also need healers in other areas of life. We need to remain hopeful and believe a better world is coming. I was promised, the best is yet to come.

MESSAGE #2
ANGELS AND GUIDES
WITH YOU

Angels and Guides are with you now more than ever. We know these times are hard and scary for most of the people of this planet. We understand the truly difficult and devastating reality you face, but from our vantage point we see things in a different way. We know the "why" this is all happening. Many of you have received guidance and messages of this transforming time, of a new awakening, that is what is happening to all of you and the whole of Earth. Not only are you as a species evolving, but all the creatures and Earth herself is changing too.

This time of awakening has been known and prophesied from long ago. Many indigenous people have known this time was coming, this change. We are rejoicing for we know the wonders that will open and be available for everyone. Not all will be ready for this change and many will be frightened and not wish to stay. Those who do not wish to stay will come home and the adjustments will happen here. When they are ready, they will come back, changed and ready for the new world. Many of you may experience strange aches and pains, even feelings of sickness. Some of these are not medical, but changes we are introducing to your bodies to help with the transformation. We are realigning you for the shift into a higher level of light and frequency. The shift into higher consciousness.

Not only are messages being sent from Heaven, but Earth herself is giving you help and guidance. She has always talked to those who listen. The ancient ones, the indigenous peoples of Earth know the language. They can talk to the animals and plants and know what plants are food or medicine and what ones are not. That language is still here and people are beginning to open, to hear it once again. Farmers will know, if they can listen, the needs of the earth they til. The harmony they have with the earth will enhance the crops they grow and therefore enhance the food we eat. People need to reconnect to earth and hear her messages.

You have never been left unattended, on the contrary, you are given much loving guidance. Do not let fear blind you to what miracles are around you. You are wrapped in a blanket of love and light. So many people are open and talking about this transformation, listen, for we speak through them. There are magnificent wonders that await you. All the tools are here for you to manifest a clean beautiful world. Use your dreams and thoughts to create the utopia you want to live in. Listen to the inner yearnings of your soul, not your mind, but deep in your soul where you feel the right path and knowledge. The more you dream and believe the faster these ideas will become real. We have stockpiles of new inventions just waiting for you to create them. Think big and don't be afraid. New alliances will be created throughout the world, everyone will learn to work and live together. It will be a more peaceful and rewarding life with less stress and a cleaner world to live in. Nature will rule, and be honored. Ask for the help and guidance you need, for we have an abundance of love to give.

INTRODUCTION TO MESSAGES #3 AND #4

When Gabriel started talking about love, he showed me what it looks like to the Angels and other advanced guides. They see it as thin iridescent threads of light. He showed me what it looks like connected throughout the universe. There were millions of thin threads connecting all the planets and stars together in this magnificent web. The light on these threads pulse and move constantly with the ever flowing light. The light is made up of all the colors like a rainbow. This is love moving throughout the universe and feeding it. Without this love we would not exist. This is the fuel, the necessary force of life.

MESSAGE #3
OTHER WORLDS

There are other worlds and entities throughout the universe, some more advanced in their thinking and actions, others not as far along. These entities vary in size and shape depending on where they live. Their planet defines the body they inhabit. The body must work with the planet's makeup. An Earth body would not work on other planets and so each body is unique to its own planet to hold the soul for the term of its journey. Many souls will visit other planets to learn and grow, humans have visited other planets to experience different lifetimes too. It is similar to how exchange students visit other countries here on Earth.

The planets and stars and all celestial bodies are a reflection of your imagination, which is part of the collective mind. Stars hold great power and force. They undulate and move to the swaying waves in the universe. Each has a unique tonal sound that it resonates to, much like a musical note. There is music that is found in the Heavens more beautiful than any on Earth. The universe is not stationary, it is in constant motion and the stars and planets move to its flow. These celestial bodies have great force, but they feel the winds of change that are happening now. All things are connected by the web of light, which is really love. This is not the internet. This web is unseen but strong and it is found throughout the universe. When it is seen through advanced eyes it looks like thin, iridescent light strands. These strands are made of love connecting all life forces together and each and every life force can feel it.

In each of you the web is strong, but many of you do not feel the pull yet. You think of yourselves as separate or alone, but all are truly only one. When one falls the vibration` is felt throughout the world. More and more of you are feeling the pull of change. You are waking to the pull of the web and feeling your interconnectedness. You feel that something is wrong and react to it. Only love will heal fear. In time you will feel when an animal is hurt or a tree falls, you were all that connected, at one time, and will be again. You are reawakening to these things, opening to the possibilities that you are growing in the truths that have always been within you. This rippling effect in the web is how you were meant to communicate and connect with others. You will be aware of more, know more, and feel more. Your vibration levels will rise and you will want change and work toward it. That's why, this time, what you feel, feels different. There is an urgency this time, to make it right. There will reach a point of critical mass where true change will happen because the collective mind sees it as so. There will always be some who will fight against the change, but for most it will become necessary.

We are helping to reconnect these bands of light, of love, in the web. This will help to enhance everyone's ability to feel the pull and know when the web has been stretched or broken. The web is growing stronger in each of you. You are being altered to see life through new eyes. Right now is a perfect time to look inside, to forgive others and yourself. To truly feel and see the magnificent being you are. To live in a state of joy as you were meant to live. You are of God, it is time you remember your true connection to Him.

MESSAGE #4
LOVE

You celebrate love on one day each year, Valentine's Day, but love should be celebrated everyday throughout the year.

Love is the fuel, the essence of all life. It courses through all living things, trees, rocks, animals and stars. In everything, everywhere there is love. It is the fuel, the energy in the web of life. Without it the web of life would be just strands connecting all living things together, but without any force. Love is the power in the web of life, without it the web is useless and does not have any purpose.

You only think of love as a romantic feeling, which it is, but it is so much more. The love I am talking about is not lust. The love that powers the universe is felt when you help a friend, care for your pet, love your family. It is power, energy and light. It fuels all living things. If a car doesn't have gas it won't run, without love the universe would collapse. It powers everything, everywhere.

Cyndi had a near death experience at age 13. When she was in God's presence she was embraced by God's love, it was poured into her. It is difficult to find words for that magnificent feeling, but in a very real way she was being refueled by God's love. God's love is the fuel that powers the universe.

Love, you can't see it, or touch it, but you can feel it. You write books and songs about it, and above all else, it is what everyone craves the most. God's love does not have any strings attached, no rules. It is given freely and completely to all. As humans you put rules, restrictions, measurements and judgements on your love. You hold love back from some, including yourselves.

Try and think of love as a fuel, it is as important in sustaining your life as water. This fuel needs to flow throughout the universe, continuously with ease. As the speed and flow increases things heal and more joy and happiness are found where before there was little. It is a healing balm. There is an abundance of God's love, it can never run dry. The faster and easier love flows out of you, the more love is returned to you. Circulation throughout the universe is critical for it helps and heals everything. As I said before, with advanced eyes, love looks like iridescent light flowing throughout the universe on thin strands that makeup the web of life. The stronger the love in you the brighter the light in you, more love, more light, you literally glow brighter.

Spread more love throughout your life, in all aspects, everyday. As you give more love you may feel your heart expanding. The more you give the more you will receive. As the love in you increases, your light grows brighter and those who are dark will find less places to hide. As the light brightens the vibrations increase in you which speeds up your transformation to higher levels of consciousness. It is a chain reaction. As the fuel, love, increases its flow it creates more light, which increases the vibration levels, which speeds up the transformation to higher levels of consciousness.

Turn up your flow and let your love, light shine.

MESSAGE #5
PATHWAYS IN THE
UNIVERSE

There are pathways throughout the universe that are like super highways, where any kind of being can speed through time and space in an instant. These super highways connect all celestial bodies and different dimensional worlds together to make travel easier. These highways can't be seen but they are felt and are known to all. On each planet, or celestial body, there are several entry points or portals. These entry points can sometimes cause disturbances in the atmospheres of planets. Here on Earth you are sometimes affected by these portals, but few know or understand what they truly are. This interconnectedness creates a beautiful musical dance of planets, stars, all celestial bodies and all of creation even in different dimensions. Everything moves to the waltz of the universe, to its flow. We are all a part of this magnificent music, all is right, we are where we should be at this moment.

All over Earth there are pathways of energy called Ley lines. This energy grid sends light and power all around Earth. These energy paths criss cross around the world and where they cross higher energy is felt. All creatures draw on Earth's energy. Some creatures use these lines for migration and others follow pathways throughout the oceans. As humans you have built buildings of worship, of all types, on these lines, especially where they cross. Independence Hall has 3 Ley lines that cross right behind it. The forefathers of your country knew about these lines and built this important building to have Earth's energy fortify those who worked there. These Ley lines are a source of great power, especially where they cross, this energy pulls all of creation to come and connect with Earth. Her energy heightens your awareness and opens your connectedness to her.

Earth is a living thing and like all living things she has energy and a soul. Your connection to Earth is intimate and real. She sustains your life while you are here. You don't think of her as alive, but she is and she cares for all creatures that live on her. In the past, people used to walk on these energy lines in bare feet or with leather shoes so they could feel and soak up Earth's energy through their feet. Gardeners sometimes feel the energy through their hands as they work the soil. Many indigenous people still know and understand Earth's energy lines. Earth's energy and flow is still felt within you, even if you are not aware of what it is. You are connected to Earth and all she is, more than you realize. For too long you have neglected and abused the resources of Earth. Now is the time for truly understanding your role and responsibilities to Earth. In this time of great change it is necessary to correct and attend to past mistakes made to Earth. As your interconnectedness grows and your vibration levels increase, know that Earth will also transform in tandem with the human race. Her needs now become important so that she can raise vibrationally with you. Help her by doing all you can to protect all of Earth's creatures as well as Earth herself. Your energies are intertwined with Earth's and can not be separated. Love and care for Earth as she has cared and loved you. You are an integral part of Earth.

MESSAGE #6
WHAT HAPPENS TO
YOU AFTER DEATH

Angels are not male or female, we have some human characteristics within each of us, but we are uniquely different from humans in many ways. We do not have families or own any properties. Our soul purpose is to serve God and help the beings of the universe find joy. We intervene when we are asked for help or assistance, but we can not act unless we are first asked. Each guardian Angel is assigned to an individual for the duration of their life, from their first breath to their last. Upon their final breath they accompany the soul of that person, back to Heaven. Each human carries a unique and precious gift in them, a tiny piece of God. This divine gem is guarded and watched over by your guardian Angel. Everything in God's universe has a soul, but only beings, like humans, have the divine spark of God within them. Even we as Angels do not carry this gift in us.

On Earth, as on other planets throughout the universe, there are beings of light and those of evil. The web of life that connects all of creation together still connects all types of beings together. It is by your choice as to what you will be. When you were in Heaven, before this life began, you made a very detailed life plan for yourself. Once you arrived on Earth all memory of that plan was erased. Your second, very special gift from God, is that of free will. You have the right to follow the plan you made for yourself or you can change it and improve upon it. You can also decide to go down a very dark, negative path that takes you away from God's love. You have the right to make new and different choices every day of your life. God's love for you doesn't stop just because you pick a different path. If you are on a negative path you are the one who has turned off the spigot to God's love and chosen to go in that direction. The negativity you find yourself in is by your own doing. If you ask for help and guidance you will be given help and the light of love will flow into you once again. No soul is forgotten or lost, God forgets no one.

When you return home after a lifetime you do not face a board of review where your life's deeds are laid out in front of you. There is no judgement panel or God sitting on a throne looking down on all you have done. Only you will review your life in its entirety. Great deeds are important, but how you treated your fellow man is of greater importance. You will feel the weight of your decisions as they were received by others. You will know, for the good or not so good, how your life's actions and deeds affected others. Then you will know, from others point of view, how you were perceived. Did you accomplish your goals? Did you learn some of the lessons you had written in your life's plan to learn? What did you gain in truths? You will have the answers to these questions and more to prepare you for your next lifetime, but only if you wish to have one.

Upon your return you will reconnect with your higher self. Not all of your soul fits into the human body. You are able to do and be so much more than you believe you can do. You can bi-locate at will, travel to any place in the universe just by thought, communicate telepathically and so much more. These limitations are necessary to live a life on Earth, but in Heaven you will remember all you truly are and embrace your true abilities. You will reconnect with loved ones, especially your pets. You have vocations in Heaven that keep you busy. It is also a time to heal, relax and regenerate. In Heaven you plan and prepare for your next course, will it be another lifetime on Earth or on a different planetary system? Perhaps you wish to be a friend's guide for their lifetime. There are so many options open to you. You will decide your next best course. Guides will help you navigate your choices, but in the end it is your decision. Where will you go? What will you be? So many paths to explore. Heaven is only the starting point for your next adventure.

We as Angels are here to help and guide. If you listen and give us the opportunity we can help you achieve your goals and wishes while on Earth. Our main job is that of assistance and reassurance. You are never without guidance or help, you are never alone. God's love is so abundant and we were created to embody that love in a useful, caring way. You may not see us or feel us, but we are always by your side, you are always in God's care and ours.

MESSAGE #7
GABRIEL'S GIFT

Knee replacement surgery was scheduled for me on April 5th. I was not scared, but I also was not looking forward to the surgery and recovery.

About 2 weeks prior to my surgery a wonderful gift arrived. I had been outside working in our yard and had come into the kitchen. As I walked in, my eyes caught something on the floor. It was a feather, mostly black with some brown on it. I thought, "I must of brought it in on my shoe". So I picked it up and placed it on our Welsh cupboard in the kitchen and forgot about it.

A week later I was cleaning up from breakfast and I walked past the cupboard and there ON the cupboard was another feather. This one was gray. It was early in the morning, we have 2 noisy dogs and no birds, and no one had been in our house, someone or something had to have put the feather there. I was now very aware that something unusual was happening.

I thought about the first feather. Both feathers are a good 4 inches long. In our house the kitchen is in the middle of the house, so to get there you have to cross our livingroom, den or come through the garage and laundry room. There is no way a feather would stick to a shoe for that distance.

Finally that afternoon I got quiet and asked Gabriel if the feathers were from him. He said yes, they were from him for "reassurance." I was stunned and humbled. What a wonderful gift.

Even as a psychic I had missed the first feather's message so he had to place the second feather where I wouldn't miss it.

I did enter surgery knowing I would be fine. I now am recovering and working on my knee strength.

Two feathers will always remind me of my Angelic connection and their sweet, persistent love.

MESSAGE #8
JOY, YOUR NATURAL
STATE OF BEING

Joy is your natural state, it is the state you were meant to live in. Yet most humans do not live in a blissful state of joy. How did you get so far from your natural state? Humans were created as perfect. God created you from love and gave you a part of divinity which you carry within you. You do not need to fix, learn, work or do anything to improve or better yourself. Perfect is perfect.

Somewhere back in time humans felt separated from God and therefore less than perfect. The decision to create lifetimes started, expanded and has continued ever since. Humans have felt that each lifetime is a chance to correct, experience, or pay back a karmic mistake. You, and you alone, have been the ones to create these illusions that these lives are real. They are not. They are your version of acting out your own desires and wishes. You create these lives to satisfy your needs and wants. You are the main character in your own play, everything is created by you to satisfy your own goals or needs. This constant lifetime after lifetime is not necessary or needed. God watches, and sees you like children playing dress up and make believe. That's what you do in each lifetime, you pretend and you play a role which feels real, but in reality it is not. They are unnecessary and in time you will understand this and wish for these to end. Only when you realize that this is self created and self imposed will you begin to question why? Why have I done this? What do I hope to learn that I haven't learned before? When you tire of this merry-go-round you will finally reach a point where you will want to understand your true identity and change. You will end the repetition and all the doubt about yourself. You will forgive yourself and others, and give into the fact that you are in fact perfect and have always been.

God waits patiently for you to surrender, and to awaken to the love that is in you. God created you from love in perfect form. There has never been a need to improve upon that. It is only in your eyes that you see yourselves as imperfect. That is where the judgement started and the separation began. God is waiting for a time when you will look at yourself and realize that you are perfect, and that perfection is your true identity. Then you will join with God in your true state of joy and live as you were meant to live.

MESSAGE #9
CHAKRAS

Your bodies are amazing. They house your soul for the duration of your life here on Earth. Long before you took your first breath, you designed your body in Heaven. You decided what you would look like, your eyes, height, and any imperfections you might have. You also decided all you would experience throughout your lifetime. You picked the time and place of your birth as well as your parents. No detail was left out. As you grew you discovered your body could and sometimes couldn't do what you wanted it to do. Perhaps you couldn't run as fast as you wanted so you exercised and worked on this skill and in time you could run faster. Your body is an amazing machine that adapts to your ever changing wishes.

The inner part of the body is made up of parts no one can see, yet they are of great importance. Chakras are like energy hubs in the body. Each chakra has a specific area to control and keep aligned. If your chakras are blocked or out of alignment then it is easier for disease to set in. Chakras help the energy/love flow from Spirit down into your Crown chakra, then down throughout your body keeping it healthy and in tune. The chakras are as follows, the Root Chakra, Sacral Chakra, Solar Plexus Chakra, Heart Chakra, Throat Chakra, Third Eye Chakra, and the Crown Chakra. These seven chakras help the healthy flow of energy or love to feed your body. Food, rest and exercise are all important, but the flow of energy/love is more important.

Your connection to spirit is important for messages and information to be imparted to you. The Crown Chakra, will receive not only energy/love, but messages from Spirit. Meditation or just getting quiet will help open yourself so the knowledge that is being sent can be received. When a friend comes by to talk to you, you sit and listen to what they have to say. As you get used to hearing Spirit speak to you, you will feel like you are communicating with a friend. In the quiet you are inviting Spirit to join in a conversation with you. You are always being given guidance and help, but to hear this information, you need to create quiet space. The more you practice this quiet listening, the easier it will be to hear Spirit's guidance. You are always changing and growing, listening with an open heart to guidance will help you achieve all you want and more.

INTRODUCTIONS TO MOTHER MARY

In May of 2021, Gabriel said I would be visited by other beings. I told him I looked forward to meeting other beings. In June I was visited by Mother Mary. Her energy is strong and powerful, but in a calm, feminine and regal way. She was softer spoken than Gabriel and she had a lot she wanted to pass along so it took 3 months to get all of her messages written. She sees herself as our mother, all of us, no matter our age or religion she feels that motherly instinct toward all of us. She is sweet, loving and kind. She feels responsible for us as a mother would and so she passed along her messages which I now give to you.

MESSAGE #10
MOTHER MARY'S
FIRST MESSAGE

Toward the end of May I was visited by Mother Mary. She imparted some messages to me. I could feel her quiet, strong feminine power. It was different from Gabriel's. She commands respect, but in a gentle way. Gabriel has asked me to share her messages starting in July.

She is our Mother to all. She wants us to trust in her, as our Mother, as she leads us to a better tomorrow by loving ourselves and others equally. Love yourself as you are with all your frailties.

As a child you were taught many lessons to do this and that, but were you given permission to love yourself as you are? Probably not, even though your parents did. You love others, but rarely love yourself with equal respect. That needs to change. By loving yourself you open yourself up to understanding who and what you truly are. You are made of love, not just flesh and bone, love is the energy that courses through you and gives you life.

This love is found throughout the universe and is the energy that runs all of life everywhere. Without love we don't exist. It is our essence. If we can tune into this love and open ourselves to it, it gets amplified and becomes greater. We then feel more, understand more and are open to grow more in our knowledge of the universal workings of God.

It's like turning on a tap of water. Little trickles turn into gushes the more the tap is turned. So it is with love. Understanding, wisdom, and knowledge will come forth when the tap is open and the love can flow.

She is our Mother and she wants to teach us how to love ourselves as we do others and all things. By opening ourselves to this love we learn to be open to others and most importantly, to the love of God.

It is not selfish or arrogant to love yourself. It is knowing, kindness and acceptance of all you are. It is the gentle, sweet knowledge of yourself, loving all aspects equally and honestly without exception. That kind of love is not pompous or self righteous, it is deep within you. It holds power and opens the tap to greater understanding to the workings of the universe and all it has to offer.

Mother Mary has great strength, just by her presence. She commands respect by being and knowing You are entitled to that respect as you know and love yourself. By opening up to that full love you become grounded in who you are, all of you. Power comes from that acceptance and grace of just being you. When you are open and clear of all old covers, and stand naked to the world, you will be stronger than ever before. This honesty will let you be free to just be you.

How wonderful would the world be if all could just be themselves and accepted for that. Peace would reign.

This is the goal Mother Mary has for us. It is obtainable for all, but it starts with opening yourself up to love. First and honestly love yourself, then love others. Realize God's love flows in each of us, therefore we are no different from one another. We were all created by love.

To honor Mother Mary, know yourself as you truly are, start to open to this love and feel it flow. As it flows changes will happen, changes are happening now. Open and accept yourself completely with love. Once you do that the rest will easily follow.

She leads us and asks us to trust her as our Mother, honor her wishes.

MESSAGE #11
MOTHER MARY'S
SECOND MESSAGE

Once you recognize the love within yourself, you will see it in everyone and everything. As you feel this love you will look at life with different eyes and never again wish harm in any way. You will see perfection in everything, everywhere.

You will not be able to see anything but the perfect love that surrounds everyone and everything. Your vision will, forever more, be changed.

It's like putting on a new set of glasses and seeing life in its true form. You will never again be able to go back to your old thoughts and habits. Your vision has changed and so has your heart. You feel and see love everywhere, in all things.

As your vision changes so does your heart and other parts of your body. Your heart is now more open and receives the additional love that is pouring in. Your senses are heightened and your body is undergoing change. Your chakras are opening and aligning into proper alignment allowing the flow of love and universal information to come into you with ease.

You are becoming an open channel for information ready to receive and understand messages from the Divine. You will be in tune with the higher realms and communication will flow easier.

As you open yourself to this expansion and information you realize how perfect God's plan is and how it all works together. So much will now be understood and this information is available to everyone, once you are aligned and open. Now you are open to communicate with higher beings, Angels and guides can all work with you so you can achieve the knowledge you want. Everything is available to you, you just have to ask for it.

Physically your body will change. You will become lighter, more at ease with yourself and the world. Many physical aches and pains will disappear. Your natural state of joy will be the normal as opposed to the exception. You will crave only natural, good food for your body and you will notice it functions at a higher, more efficient level.

Sleep will come easier and remembering your dreams will become easier too. Many times messages are delivered in this dream state.

Resentments and past disagreements with others will seem childish and unimportant.

They will not matter and that eases your heart and overall health too. You will not carry all the heaviness of anger within you and that will change your body for the better. Tensions will lessen and ease throughout your body, allowing the strain in muscles and joints to disappear. Many diseases will just go away and you may feel more youthful again. Disease is "unease" within you. As you become filled with love the "unease" will go away.

Your relationships with others will improve as you see them as yourself through eyes of love. You will not judge and criticize but instead look, understand and accept. This will not happen in an instant, but as you open the tap of love and let it fill you, you will see and feel significant change.

For others who are not yet ready to open to this love you will seem different, even strange. You will accept this, knowing in time they also will go through this change. You may even lose friendships because of how you now feel and act. That's OK, they will be back once they understand and start down this path of change too. Never fear loss, it is only temporary, nothing is ever really lost.

Be kind to yourself and others as you go through this change. It will take time to adapt to the new you and others will need time to adjust too.

In the end your body will be grateful for the change, even if you are not sure about the new you. Losing an old identity can be hard and scary. Be brave and know a new and better you will emerge, happier and stronger than before.

MESSAGE #12
MOTHER MARY'S
THIRD MESSAGE

Forgiveness is important. First, forgive yourself for all past deeds, for all your short-comings and imperfections. Start with yourself and honestly go within to forgive all.

Once you can honestly and openly forgive who you are for all past and present things, then it is time to forgive anyone who you have not forgiven and need to. Go back and search them out, even if it is only in your mind. You don't have to face them in person, but you do need to honestly, from the heart, forgive them.

As this load gets lifted you will feel lighter and more at peace within yourself. Daily prayer or meditation will help keep you grounded and in touch with the Divine. How and where you meditate is not important, but doing it is.

This keeps these channels open so the flow of information can come through easier. The more you are open the easier these messages can get through. As you get use to this prayer/meditation it will become an integral part of your day. And just like exercise you will feel the need to keep it up for your body and soul.

Honor yourself and don't get upset if there are setbacks. If you have a hard time releasing anger toward your cousin or co-worker, realize it takes time and work. It doesn't magically happen at once. Work on each one slowly and as you make progress notice how you feel, lighter, less tension, happier.

Now the next step is loving yourself unconditionally. You love parts of yourself. If you are an athlete you love your strength or speed and you work hard to stay in top form, but loving the parts of you you don't like is hard, I don't like the fact that I am losing my hair, I am fat, I judge people quickly, I have little patience, I get angry at what others have and I don't. The list is endless and complex, but if one at a time you look at each of these and can overcome the anger and fear, one by one they can fall away.

It takes time and commitment and you can't get frustrated that you feel it is taking too long. Each step is a milestone and one more burden you can put down and not carry anymore. Be free of these dislikes and move toward acceptance of all. This is not an easy task, but a necessary and important one. This is your task to take one part at a time, examine it, understand it, and release it with love. Examine each aspect, really look at it from all angles, know why it is there and where it came from. What started it? Can it now be let go? Then release it with love.

Over and over again one at a time look at each aspect, and you will uncover some hard truths about yourself along the way, if you are honest. There is no judgement, no one is watching you, it is only you being honest with yourself. This is not easy to do. As you release each piece give yourself a victory dance, a high five. One part honestly examined and released, these are big steps, celebrate each one. The more you do the better you will feel and you will find the task not as burdensome. Some will be very hard to face, be brave, these milestones will help you in the long run.

You are never totally without fault, but you can lighten your load. That is because you don't see yourself as perfect, even though you are. Accept that the more work you do the better you will feel. Learn to love yourself as you are truly loved.

INTRODUCTION TO JESUS

When Jesus came through it was like I was plugged into a high voltage wire. He came with so much energy it took me days to recover. His transfer of energy was like nothing I had ever encountered before. He apologized to me and told me he was responsible for this, but said I would recover, which I did a few days later. His energy was large and all encompassing, but very compassionate. When he started to talk and deliver his message his tone softened and he talked more quietly about surrender. This is word for word his message, I edited nothing in this message.

MESSAGE #13
JESUS' MESSAGE ON SURRENDER

Toward the end of July I was visited by Jesus. He has very strong, powerful energy. I felt like I was holding a high voltage wire, I was filled with His strong energy for days. He told me the energy I felt was from Him and He apologized for the power of it. He did say in time it would wear off and it has. This message, He passed on to me and asked me to pass it on to others.

Surrender, the word sounds like you are losing your identity, giving up, failure. It sounds very negative, but nothing can be further from the truth. In reality you are part of a whole, the whole being God. Therefore you really don't exist as an individual. I know this may sound strange, but this is the truth. Surrender is not giving up or giving in, but realizing what and who you truly are, it is a part of something much bigger.

Surrender is knowing that you are a part of God and therefore perfect in every way. You don't have flaws and defects and you don't need to pay back karmic debts. These you've invented because you feel less than perfect, less than God. But being a part of God makes you perfect and complete, you just don't remember. By finally surrendering to God you will be reunited and truly know yourself as you honestly are.

God's plan is perfect and once you can see it you will understand your place in it. You will know what you wrote for this lifetime and why and you will understand all your struggles and work and disappointments are unnecessary. Perfect is perfect, you don't need to fix anything. Remembering your true self may seem hard and a long stretch, especially if you feel unworthy of God's love. But I assure you, you were not meant to work or struggle so hard at life.

Life is meant to be joyful and happy. So few of you experience life this way. You don't know your true self and who and what you really are. You think of yourself as flesh, not spirit and soul. You feel grounded to Earth, not of the stars and the universe. Once you can start to look up and see and feel yourself as more than mortal, you will begin to open to who you truly are. Be brave and know that you have lived hundreds of times all unnecessary to improve yourself. You truly have one identity and that is known to you and God. You were made perfect by God, no additional upgrades are needed.

Start to learn about your true self in connection to God. Once you start to seek this identity all else will seem unimportant. Open to God's love and let it fill and feed you. For His love is the food of the universe and all need and crave it. Open to God, look for understanding of His perfect plan and realize you have a place in that plan just for you. You all are needed just as you are.

Surrendering to God is not giving up your identity, it is finding your place next to God, filled with His love. It is not weakness but strength, it takes strength of character to open yourself up to fully surrender. That is the definition of true faith. Fear can't enter into your thoughts only love. Only the strong can open and believe enough to be that vulnerable.

Believe in God's love, know it is real and know it is the sustaining power that holds the universe together. Without God's love all life would cease to exist. With a force that powerful you would think everyone would want to be filled with love, but so many are lacking faith and are afraid.

Be not afraid, God's love is here for all, in abundance for all to have. Fill yourself and be made new.

MESSAGE #14
POWER

Power, people want it, crave it, and will do anything to get it. Power is force, control, and distinction, but such power can be seductive and a trap within itself. There is nothing wrong with power, but it is all the side effects that are degrading and hurtful. With power comes prestige and the feeling you are better than most. You control something and you can make people do as you want.

True power is none of these. True power gives others the ability to choose for themselves. It lets others share in the glory and the dividends. It lets others find their way to the top, even if it is above you. It rejoices as others gain in their own success.

Real power is not boastful or arrogant, it does not demand anything of anyone. It opens doors for others to explore their ideas and gives them power to soar and fly. True power gives it back to others so all can gain and prosper, not just one.

It's not a top down way of looking at things, it's across the board even for all, giving everyone their share of the credit and profit.

True power is even, quiet, open, encouraging and supportive of others. This power doesn't have to boast or wear it outwardly for all to see. It is humble and quiet and blends in with others, just one of the many, not special.

When you gain this power, in whatever field you pursue, you don't need a megaphone to proclaim yourself. You are quiet and proud of all who have contributed to your rise. They deserve a chance to share in the goals and dreams and have some of the rewards too.

True power is found inside, in the peace within you. When you can look at others and see yourself in them, then you have touched on true power. It is not outward rewards, it is inner growth. This growth of oneself is to gain knowledge and help others along their path. When true inner power is found it shines forth from a person. Others can feel it, sense it and usually want to be around that person.

Jesus holds great inner power. He was not a successful business man and He didn't make lots of money, but people followed Him because of His inner power. They listened to His words and felt the truth in them, and still do today.

No sacrifice is being asked of you, only that you use your power for the good of all. Use your voice and influence to heal and help others. Instead of false exterior lights, let your real inner light shine, your true power. When that power shines all can feel it. Use this power to help others and you will know true power in all you do.

MESSAGE #15
ANGELS ARE YOUR
CHEERLEADERS

Angels are the cheerleaders in the game of life.

We communicate with you in dreams, intuition and that gut feeling you sometimes have. In this time of high anxiety we communicate with many, like Cyndi, who are open and can easily receive our information. Most of you are so wrapped up in your lives you miss simple signs we send you. We try to warn you if there is danger or help you achieve your goals. Nothing happens by luck.

From the moment of your birth we have been with you and will be with you to accompany you home, in the end. In between we try to help and guide you to achieve all you wish out of life. Most of you are too busy to stop and hear us. Many think of us as living long ago in stories that don't relate to today. And some think we are not real at all.

We are real, just as you are, but we live in a different dimension, so we can not be seen by most. We were created by God to assist you in these lives. But since most or many don't believe in us we are left without means to really do what we were commissioned to do. We can't fulfill our job. Some, like Cyndi, do use us to assist her in her daily life. She had a mole removed from her back last week, but instead of having to wait 7 days to hear from her doctor if it was dangerous, we told her that she had nothing to worry about. That gave her peace of mind. She will ask us about where to find an item she wants to buy as a gift for someone and we tell her what store to find it in. Our skills are not limited to just life or death decisions. We can be helpful in daily life too. If you get used to talking to us on a daily basis, then when major events happen, you will know our voice and be more willing to reach out for our additional help.

Finding time to just get quiet is not always easy but it is the best way to open the flow of communication between us. You don't need anything special to start the conversation, just talk and we will hear you. God is always watching and has sent us to help. You think of yourselves as imperfect and therefore not worthy of God's love. Your individual traits give you strengths and some weaknesses too, but they make you unique and these characteristics add to the fabric of existence. Without you the fabric is incomplete, each of you is necessary.

Open yourself to the quiet and let us help. There are no contracts, we do not hold any power over you and you don't have to follow our advice. We are open, objective, silent partners and our goal is to help you. Many fears will disappear once you realize we are real. We may not live in your world, but we work here.

We are on call 24/7 and you don't even need a phone to reach us.

Yes, we are found in the old stories and in ornaments on Christmas trees but we are alive now, today. We have perfect vision and can help you avoid the potholes of life.

You were never meant to travel this life alone. Believe in our existence and take that leap of faith with us.

MESSAGE #16
CHANGING YOUR TUNE

It is here, the change, the evolution of your soul. You are standing on the precipice, each of you choosing to be here, to witness, and be a part of this transformation. Rejoice, it is happening! Radical change is occurring, but not to everyone at once. Look around and know that all is in flux, evolving. Change is uneasy and not comfortable, but so necessary and exhilarating. Don't greet this with anger or fear, greet this with joy and excitement. Your interconnectedness to all of life is growing and is much greater than you think. As you evolve and transition forward you will begin to know how others feel, you will understand more than ever before. Nature is part of this evolution, interconnected to each of you in the web of life. You may not be aware of it yet, but you will.

You are all getting reprogrammed to be more sensitive, more intuitive, to know we are really only one. This realignment or change is happening now. The vibrations of the world are rising. If you pay attention you can see and feel the change happening. People are making real environmental changes. Racial injustice is not being tolerated by people of all colors. People are standing up for real change and true justice. It will take time, but the wave has started and it will not stop. The energy has shifted and many wrongs will no longer be tolerated.

You are energy, energy vibrates, vibrations create sound, sound creates tone and tone can create music. Your music is changing, rising to the new vibrational levels of the universe. The higher your vibrations the more you can feel. Your feelings come from deep in your soul. Music is the sound of your soul, which sings to God.

As you increase your level of understanding and open to the complexities of life your vibration levels rise, you start to add more instruments to your music. You hear and feel the different tonal abilities of each soul. It becomes an orchestra of life. Each living thing resonates to its own sound or tone, no two are alike. The web of life vibrates with each individual frequency. Your sound or frequency is like no other, and for many of you, your tune is changing. You will resonate to a new sound or frequency, higher than before.

The music found throughout the universe is diverse, intense and immense. As your frequency grows you will be immersed into life with greater intensity. It is not just understanding more, but actually feeling more deeply down to the marrow of your soul. Life will get magnified, injustices will hurt deeper, beauty will bring you to tears. All of life will be heightened. Yet there is still so much more to learn and know.

This growth will bring you closer to understanding what it means to really be one, to know you are loved, cherished and part of the Whole. Space is not filled with empty quiet, it is filled with rivers of music flowing throughout the cosmos. In this season of wonder when miracles seem more possible and kindness comes a little easier, open yourself to God's love, and embrace the rising frequency within you. The universe is waiting for you to open your heart and soul so you can hear and feel the music. Your music is changing, rejoice, and get ready to sing a new tune.

INTRODUCTION TO METATRON

In January of 2022, I heard a different voice, a deeper voice than Gabriel's, talking to me and he introduced himself as Metatron who is an angel. I had not talked to him before, he said he had a message to pass along and asked if I would be willing to listen and add it to my other messages. I told him I happily would so here is Metatron's message on kindness.

MESSAGE #17
KINDNESS

You are magnificent beings! Created from stardust and moonbeams and stirred together with God's love. You are celestial beings full of light, grace and power, yet you rarely use these attributes. Your power is unparalleled, but you had to forget your true identity in order to live here on Earth. Giving up so much is the only way you could live as a human on this difficult Earth school. But inside you is your true identity and balancing that against your human traits is a difficult task. Remembering who you truly are is part of your lessons here on Earth. Understanding that you are so much more than this mortal shell is a necessary goal. Kindness seems easier for you to give when you are helping a friend, or being nice to a stranger. You smile and open a door or let someone cut in line in front of you. You donate money to people you don't even know because a tornado destroyed their home. Simple acts of kindness ripple out and affect others in ways you may never know. Tolerance for others does not mean you have to agree with them, it just means you accept them, with grace, as a fellow human. You may not agree with what they stand for, but they should be allowed the same rights as you to live life as they wish. This discord creates harmony in life. Kindness seems easier for you to give to others rather than yourself. Why is that? Why is it so hard to see your goodness?

You see yourself as imperfect, yet we know differently. God sees sweetness, compassion, love and so much more. You are not this one person in this one lifetime, you are a collection of all the lives you have lived and a total of all lives others have lived too. You are never just one person, you are all. Each one of you is a part of all. When God creates it is always perfect. Self love is important for your emotional, physical and spiritual well being. How you feel about yourself impacts all aspects of your life and others too. If you are full of self love you have love to give to others. If you are empty you have nothing to offer. Caring for yourself is not a selfish act, it is an act of kindness, and it impacts and elevates everyone.

Thoughts are the energy building blocks of your reality. As you think of something new and wonderful it starts to take on power. The more you think about it or verbally talk about it, the stronger it starts to become. The universe was set up to answer your requests, your thoughts. This thought power starts to manifest and become your physical reality If you live in a happy state of mind then positive and kind is what is designed for you. Your thought energy creates everything in your life. It is a very powerful force.

Focus on the good, the positive gains you've made, this will propel you forward. Once the momentum starts it will gain speed and there will be no stopping it. The more kindness and good that is done, the more kindness and good will be created. Wonderful things are happening all around the world, focus on them and let their momentum move you forward. Ask for help from your Angels when you are in need. We are ready to aid at any time. You think of us as floating in the ethereal, yet this is not so. We walk beside you throughout your life. We know all you endure and we try to help whenever we can.

Open your heart and find your true self again. See yourselves as these beautiful, magnificent creatures that God has created and loves. Your kindness can transform Earth into a paradise, today.

MESSAGE #18
OTHER WORLDS

Earth is just one tiny world that is inhabited. There are billions of other worlds with life on them. Some of these beings from other planets have visited Earth, others have no desire to come here.

There are entities that live in harmonious unity, working for the good of all by working as one unit. They have one mindset, one goal. There are other beings that live in consciousness only. They require no form or substance to live. There is another world where they have destroyed most of their planet through conflicts and they now live peacefully in a domed area on their planet because that is all that is left to live on. Some beings live inside their planet's surface, others live on water-like planets and some are just small dots of lights like fireflies. Some planets don't have any moons, others have many. Many planets are solid but some are made of vapor and still have inhabitants. Some beings need oxygen and water, others need nitrogen and sulfuric acid and some live in a vacuum. The makeup of each planet differs as much as the beings who inhabit them. Despite all the differences you are all more alike than different.

Many entities are more advanced than humans and they no longer have conflicts. They measure power through beauty, grace and knowledge. Many higher entities have tried to help lesser worlds to grow. These guardian planets have given help to many planets for their advancement. Earth has had help like this from other beings from other planets throughout its history. Help has been given in many forms to those who request it. Beings from different planets also live in diverse dimensions. Not all creatures live in the same dimension. Just as Earth is moving from the 3rd to the 5th dimension there are others who are living in higher and lower dimensions than Earth. Humans have lived many lives as have other creatures throughout the universe. As humans you have the ability to bi-locate, although you rarely use it. You have the ability to travel to your other lives because they are all happening at once. Many of these lives were on other planets, just as other beings have had lifetimes here on Earth.

Time is an illusion. Every life of every entity is happening at the same instant, regardless of what dimension it is happening. So there are overlapping lives of beings living on many different planets in different dimensions happening simultaneously. The goal for all is to grow and learn, to gain knowledge of who and what you truly are, to gain greater understanding of the workings of God and the universe. The universe is so vast it is incomprehensible. God keeps creating so the universe keeps growing and expanding in all directions. Your scientific world is trying to understand the boundaries of the universe, but there are none because it is infinite.

Angels travel by telepathy throughout the universe to wherever we are needed. We can be in many places at one time, we bi-locate. You have this power and you will use it more as you advance. Many enities travel the universe on universal pathways. These pathways speed an entity or vehicle to other galaxies in an instant. To gain this speed and distance they dematerialize, once they reach their destination they rematerialize again. Some worlds remain shut and don't wish to venture out. There are so many unique and wonderful entities in this universe, yet most of you have so little knowledge of any of them. When you meet them will you be frightened or excited? Will you extend your hand in friendship? These beings may look different and communicate differently but all have been created by God.

Most of you have been schooled or had lifetimes on other planets. There are beings from other planets here now, having a human life, here on Earth. To exist on Earth a being must wear a human body in order to survive and grow. The same is true if you spend a lifetime on another planet, you wear the body that is needed for existence on that planet while you are there.

God's expansion is ongoing. Change is constant. Regardless of all the differences, we are really only one. The only constant is the love from God that threads its way through all beings and creatures. It connects all stars, planets and any other celestial body to God. Love is the binding force connecting all, throughout the universe. Love is the invisible light we all need from God, without it we cease to exist. So many unique and wondrous worlds exist and God knows each being intimately by name. We are all God's creations and He is as close to each of us as a whisper.

INTRODUCTION TO JESUS'S SECOND MESSAGE

In February of 2022, Gabriel pushed me to create a blog where all the messages were posted. I was starting something new with the blog and this opened the door for people everywhere to read these messages. In February Jesus came back with a new message which became my March message. Again I didn't edit it. His messages seem perfect just as they are.

MESSAGE #19
DEATH IS A
TRANSITION

When I was on the cross, I wanted people to understand that death is not the end, it is only a transition to something better and different. I was going home.

Death is a transition and when you have finished with a lifetime it is time to move on. You may be 2, 10 or 102, but when you are done it ends. However your soul never ends, it cannot die, it lives on for eternity. You are a part of God, therefore you can never die. Each lifetime is a learning experience full of chances to expand and grow. You need to take advantage of these times and really grow in your understanding of who and what you really are. Are you only flesh and blood? No, that is only the outer covering, it is what you are inside your soul, that matters.

Look inside and realize you have been here before, many, many times. Each lifetime is different, but each one allows you to learn and grow. Tap into your memory, and open to thoughts about other places and events. You may be drawn to an area or country, or you may be pulled to a different time in history. Pay attention to these, they are giving you clues as to who you were and where you have lived before. All of your past lifetimes have helped to create who you are today. You have lived on other planets too. Stop spinning around in your little circles and look beyond your tiny world. There is so much more to know about yourself. You have tremendous powers and abilities yet you stumble along as if blind. All of you have psychic abilities but so few of you use them. Stretch yourself, use your psychic abilities to really connect to the higher worlds. Your true identity is made from the ethers, it is God given and therefore holy. This body of yours holds your soul, or part of it, while you are here on Earth. You are a celestial body with powers you only dream about. Your powers are real and you can use them if you practice and try. Using your psychic abilities will open pathways to higher worlds and connect you with higher beings, the information you will obtain will expand you beyond all you can imagine.

I came to Earth to teach about God and his love, but also to tell you, you are so much more than you think you are. It matters not if you believe one way or another as long as you don't bring harm to others. All religions have some element of truth and falsehood, no one religion rises to the top.

Death is a doorway into your next chapter of experiences. It is as natural as breathing, yet you fear it and try to prevent it. Nothing can stop it and yes, you will be missed, but you carry fear for no reason. You will all be united again in Heaven. No one is ever lost. If you could take the fear out of death you could truly live. So much effort is spent on preventing death you miss out on living. While you can, live life to the fullest everyday. Enjoy, celebrate all you are and be joyful. Joy is the natural state of the soul, not fear. Wouldn't it be wonderful to live in that state? You can if you choose to do so. I came to show you that death is not the end, just a new beginning. Accept that it will come and enjoy life while you can. There is so much more to see and do than to get bogged down in petty things here on Earth.

Open your mind and heart to all the possibilities. Ask for guidance and it will be given. You are so much more than a body stumbling around on Earth. Greet each day with excitement and gratitude. And with grace, accept that in time each of you will pass through the doorway back home. Let fear be in your past and live now with gusto. You are always watched, guided and most of all loved. Be brave, you are always in God's hand,

MESSAGE #20
BEINGS OF LIGHT

You are beings of light, holy, created by God, to experience and grow in your wisdom and understanding of the universe and its magnificent.

The human body is a marvelous machine, designed to function while you are here on Earth. It is the vessel that holds your soul, nothing more or less.

In heaven, before you were born into this life, you picked your body like you would a suit of clothes. You chose your parents and decided where and when you wanted to be born. All decisions were made before you took your first breath on Earth. For your soul you decided what you wished to learn and work on. Some of you feel you have karmic debt to repay. You are without sin so this is not necessary, but many feel they need to balance a past wrong. All these decisions were made as to how and when they will happen in your life. Important people who are necessary in your life are also woven into the plan, like mentors and those you might call evil or mean. You asked your closest friends to take these difficult roles. They care about you, and even though you won't remember them once you are here on Earth, they agree to do this for your benefit. Some friends agree to come for only a short time and then leave. They do this to help you or others around you. Others choose to come with difficulties such as disease or physical ailments. Those that choose these are usually more advanced souls, they understand the difficulties that they will face. They do it for the good of others. The lessons of these higher souls are here for all to learn and grow.

A soul needs nourishment, not food and water but love, guidance and reassurance as it grows and reaches toward its true identity and purpose. Earth has great power and she gives it freely to all, her energy can heal and feed your soul. What the soul learns and how it reacts and feels is of paramount importance. The love that is given and received is what is truly important to the soul's growth. Love is one thing that stays with you upon death. The body is just a shell, it's what is inside that counts. The soul knows this is a temporary existence and its job is to understand and learn all that transcends time and space. The veil is thin and all the answers can be found in you, if you ask the right questions. Angels and guides in the higher realms are here waiting to help. They want to help you remember your soul's purpose and your true identity. They want to help you remember who you've been before, lessons from past lives and what you hope to accomplish in this life. Perhaps none of your goals will be met, perhaps you will pick a totally new path to explore. Perhaps you will get all your questions answered. The choice is always yours.

God can only create perfection, that fact can never change. In God's eyes you are always perfect. As we look down on Earth we see only the light in each of you, we see your soul. As your soul grows in understanding it shines brighter. And that love from within you radiates to all life everywhere. The brighter your light the more it radiates out into the world. A soul's brightness tells of one's growth and grace. While you sustain your outer body, work on your inner light. Walking in nature will help nurture and speak to your soul. Understand the power of quiet meditation. In the quiet, doors to higher realms are easily opened and information is passed along. Love and honor yourself, for in doing so you give thanks to God, for the soul God created just for you.

MESSAGE #21
YOUR AURA

Your soul does not completely fit inside your body. Some of your soul remains in Heaven in what you call your higher self. Much of it is here inside of you but the part that overflows your body is called your aura.

Your aura is your first line of defense. It can pick up intrusions into your space long before your other senses kick in. It extends out about 6 feet from your core, but this can vary. If someone or something enters that field you "feel" it. As you become more intuitive with your body and soul you can use this outer layer to help you ward off disease and alert you to any danger that is near.

Your aura is seen as a color field. If you could see the colors you could read someone's aura. The colors indicate the state of your body and mind. If your aura shows lots of red then that suggests stress, anger, fear, sadness or disease. Colors can also tell where there are issues in the body. If darkness shows up in a body part it could indicate disease is possibly centered there. Green means you are in your heart and more at peace within yourself.

You feel with these outer bands more than you know. If you are at a party and someone walks in, even if you don't see that person, you may feel a change in the atmosphere. The person could be full of light and fun and add an additional charge of happy energy to the party or a negative person could enter and the whole party could suffer from the energy that person brings. You are made of energy and wherever you go you leave traces of your energy behind. Some of you can "feel" the energy of places better than others. But each of you has this ability.

You may meet a person for the first time and have an immediate connection to them, it could be positive or negative. Most likely you are remembering them from another lifetime. Your soul's energy signature just connected to theirs. We change looks with each lifetime, but your soul's energy does not change. Your soul carries memories of each lifetime you've had and these accumulated lifetime memories make up the current you. Their accumulated effect helps to create who you currently are and how you react in different situations. Those past lifetime memories are just as alive in you now as your current lifetime memories are.

Auras can help keep disease out of your body if you keep your body healthy and clean. It can repel many diseases at the outer layers if it is healthy and strong. Once it breaks down then disease can enter more easily. Dis-ease is just what it says, your body is not at ease or at peace within itself. Your inner peace and balance play such a huge part in keeping you healthy.

As you grow in your spirituality your vibration levels increase. For most of you these levels have been rising and they will continue to rise. As your vibration levels rise many of you can aid others just by being in close proximity to them. The higher vibration levels in your aura rub off and assist others as they take in these higher levels of vibrations.

Your soul is remarkably strong and can withstand so much. It can't be killed, but it can be hurt and weakened. Honor your soul, this magical part of you that makes you unique. Care for your body and strive for the peace that will keep you in balance. As you stay in balance and grow, higher levels of communication are easily opened to you. Never forget you are a remarkable, enlightened and everlasting being.

MESSAGE #22
MANY LIVES

The reason for multiple lives is to learn and grow, to experience a vast variety of situations created through different lives lived in multiple realms and on many different planets.

You have been created "perfect" from God's hands, yet most wish to still experience a variety of different lives on many different worlds. As you live all these lives God is experiencing these many facets through you.

As I have stated before there are thousands of other planets where you can choose to go and have a lifetime. Your "body" will be unique to that world's atmospheric conditions, therefore you would not be in "human" form. You take the necessary form to adapt and live on that planet for that lifetime.

Most of you have had multiple lifetimes here on Earth. Your memory is wiped clean before each new lifetime begins, but you still carry memories of each lifetime within you. Trauma in a lifetime is usually strong and will carry over from one lifetime to the next. Triggers can sometimes unlock these hidden memories and emerge into a lifetime where it doesn't belong. For example you may have a great fear of water, yet you have no basis for this fear. Perhaps in another lifetime you drowned and so you carry that trauma with you now. You may visit a new place and feel immediately at home there. You probably lived a life in that area. Many clues to some of your lives can be uncovered if you pay attention to your inner feelings about people and places. Your soul stores all memories just as it does memories from your current life. Major events leave lasting marks on your soul both good and bad. A trigger could be a smell, an event, a place or a person. Any one of these could bring up a memory from another life. All these lives add into who you are now. Other lives are never wiped away, only stored away but never forgotten.

You talk about past lives yet all your lives are happening at once. There is no time, past or future, only now. What you feel happened in another time is currently happening just as all your lives are, you are just plugged into this life so the other lives seem distant. Time is a hard concept to understand, but it really doesn't exist as you think it does. There are also multiple dimensions, which you have lived in, so all your lives are happening in different places, in different dimensions all at once.

Many of you feel you have karmic debt you need to correct. You may feel you have done a misdeed and need to fix it. In God's eyes you can do no wrong, but many of the lives you construct are done so around karmic reasons. Lifetimes are learning tools, much like school. You come to experience different realities. During your lifetimes on Earth you have lived in many different countries, you have been different races, religions, both male and female and different sexual orientations. You choose your parents and the timing of your birth just as you add in your exit points for your departure. You put in 3 or 4 of them, then choose when the time arises. You travel with many members of your family and friends from one lifetime to the next, but all of you change roles in each lifetime. Some of you have lived lifetimes as a "famous" person, but for most of your lives you have been just everyday folks. Each life plan is very detailed and includes karmic roles if agreed upon as well as what areas you feel need work. Then this plan is reviewed by the counsel before you start a new life.

It is difficult to live on Earth. Staying on one's path is not easy to do here. Many people get lost or off track and find themselves in challenging situations. Earth is hard and a lot of consideration has to be made before coming here. It is a planet where you can progress very quickly, if you can stay on your plan. Souls can be hurt and scarred, but not killed. Very difficult and traumatizing lifetimes can leave a soul in need of cocooning when it passes over. Cocooning is caring for the soul till it is healed and ready to resume its life again.

After a difficult life a soul may want a break and agree to be someone's guide. To be a guide a soul must have had at least one lifetime on that planet and be chosen by the soul that is going into a body to be their guide. You are also assigned an angel to stay with you throughout your lifetime. You are never alone, even though at times you may feel that way. Advanced souls choose very difficult lives. They are doing this, many times, for the good of another soul, to help them. Sometimes they choose a life with a disease or disability or to live in a traumatic situation.

There are also walk-ins. A walk-in has made an arrangement prior to birth with another soul to switch places at a preselected time and place. The reason for this is that this advanced soul does not wish to go through the early years of growth into adulthood. It has a mission to complete and wants to enter when the person is grown. It usually, but not always, happens during some medical event. Perhaps the person is in the hospital for a minor procedure and it is at that time the switch happens. The new soul has all the memories of the person and looks the same, but many times friends and family see the person as somehow "different". After the switch is made the new soul is ready to pursue the work it agreed to.

Life is really a game. You design the rules and players and play out your game. In reality we are all one. And what you see is not real. These are hard concepts to grasp. As you try to understand this true reality you are taking a step closer to knowing your real soul. Each lifetime is a learning opportunity, take advantage of all that is available to you to stretch yourself and really seek to understand the true universal complexities. The shift is here and the higher realms are open to you. Ask and realize that all are here, ready to help and assist in your growth and understanding. Be open and inquisitive, you are magnificent beings full of light and love.

MESSAGE #23
AKASHIC RECORDS

The Akashic Records are found in a beautiful building in Heaven called the Hall of Records. It is a library where anyone can go and look up their own lives or that of any other soul. These records are not just books, these records go back to the beginning of time and list every detail of every life each soul has lived and so much more. They are a written record of God's knowledge, laws and memories of each planet in the entire universe. Earth's records are written in the ancient language of Aramaic.

The library gives great detail as to where a soul originated, not all of us came from Earth, many of us came from other planets originally. It talks about the lives you have had on Earth as well as lives you have had on other planets. It details your goals and purposes in each lifetime and provides an account of every life.

These records can be accessed at any time. Your life really is an open book. This library has a purpose besides being a record keeper of all lives and deeds. It offers a place to discover information about yourself or others, as well as universal information. In understanding your lives and what you have done it may offer a better explanation as to why you are the person you are. It can also do the same for others that you may be having difficulty with. By knowing who they were and the lives they have lived, it will shine a light into the makeup of that person now. The records stand for all time.

Many people have the ability to remote view the contents of these records. Some people can view them while dreaming and others can access them through meditation. It takes practice to learn to remote view, but these records were created as a tool to help in your growth and education.

Once you are in the Hall of Records you only have to think and telepathically the records are given to you. Much understanding is gleaned from knowing yourself better and perhaps others too. All of your memories are returned to you once you return to Heaven. Erasing past lives is necessary when starting a new life on Earth. This gives you a clean slate to experience a new existence in each lifetime. Your memories are still with you, just not as easily accessible. Discovering these other lives can be exciting and very informative.

In most of your lives you were just everyday folks. Sometimes you are asked to take on a larger role that puts you into the spotlight of the world. By accepting this larger role you agree to help, in some way, to guide mankind on its journey.

It could be a role that is "good" or it could be a role that is "evil". Both are needed sometimes for change to truly happen. There have been influential people throughout history. Most of us have been a "famous" person at least once, but famous or average each lifetime is important and gives you the opportunity to uncover the truths of the universe and its makeup. These lifetimes are a game you play and are not easy to understand.

As you get closer to uncovering your true identity your ego will become frightened of its extinction, but in truth we are really only one. The shift is happening and humankind will forever be changed. Your everlasting soul will continue on forever as long as God continues to spin this magnificent universe in the palm of His hand.

MESSAGE #24
LOVE/LIGHT

Prayers are released as small streams of light shooting upward toward Heaven. The more intense the prayers the brighter they shine. The brightest ones usually come from Mothers. The light that shines in these prayers, that is attached to them, is love. The more love, the brighter the prayer. The brightest prayers are answered first, but all prayers are answered.

When you are around friends and family the light within you grows and as you embrace you give some of your light/love to the other person, there is an exchange of love/light. The higher your vibration levels are, the brighter you glow. When you are low in energy your light is dimmer.

We all need and feed on love/light. Without it we can not and will not survive. Love/light is the source from which we are made. We came from God, which is 100% love/light. Each of us was created from that love/light, therefore we carry God's love/light within us. Upon our creation we all glowed with God's love/light, we were filled with it. Over lifetimes we have lost some of our love/light. We have given it away by feeling unworthy and therefore diminished. Traumas have also erased some of our love/light. Our glow is not as bright as it once was. The good news is it can be restored and refilled. There is an endless supply of love/light in the universe, because it is the fuel that runs everything. Planets spin, stars shine all because of God's love/light. It is the universal fuel.

All creation was created from this love/light and all creatures are born full of this love. They literally glow with it. Each stone, or blade of grass glows with light/love yet we can't see it. We consider nature separate from us, yet we are really all connected together. Your eyes can't see the glow or love/light within a person or creature, but you can feel it. You can feel the love/light from a child or pet, that unconditional adoring love. That is what God's love/light is, pure, adoring and unconditional. There are no strings attached or requests needed to receive it, it is there for all.

Through our eyes we see the love/light in each of you and in all creation. Many of you shine so brightly and others are in need of more love/light. You give and receive love/light all the time. When you smile at a stranger, that small exchange can help a person who is low on love/light fill up and feel better about their life. Small gestures of kindness have a great ripple effect on many. What happens to one radiates out and affects others.

In Heaven when a person passes over from a traumatic lifetime or very suddenly they sometimes need help before they can accept and move on. In these cases a soul is cocooned for a while so healing can take place. Much of the healing happens with God's love/light. That healing love/light penetrates and restores a soul.

Light is needed for your sight, for in total darkness your eyes don't work, you can not see. Light is also needed to seek inward paths to find universal answers. Love/light heals. Never forget how powerful and strong you are. You are filled with God's love/light; it is the most powerful force in the universe.

MESSAGE #25
BELIEVE

Two years ago I took Cyndi forward about 25 years to show her the future of Earth. There is much to be excited and hopeful about. Renewable energy will be in world wide use, and most oil and gas products will be gone. Universal medicine will be established for most around the world. The poor will have more food and shelter thanks to a small food tax that most nations will implement as a way to stem poverty.

Coalitions from almost every nation will work for the betterment of the Earth and all who inhabit her. Nature will rule and Earth's welfare will come first in most decisions over profits. Homes will be hubs of happiness where most people will work, some may even school from home. Governments will work together on disarmament and scaling down armies.

Not all countries will want to join but most will and the ones who don't will lose much of their influence and power. There will be a better balance throughout the world and more trust. Many wrongs will be exposed and righted. Earth will be a more peaceful planet, and most will work to maintain that peace and balance.

Food will be organic and healthy for all. Most processed and fast foods will disappear, because of their unhealthy nature. Cities will be smaller and more green spaces will pop up in them. Most businesses will have workers working from home, so some office buildings will be shared by many different businesses to use when needed. Life will be more relaxed for all.

To get to this outcome all must be willing to make changes. Start in your homes with your energy, simplify your life, and reduce your waste. Cars are now being made with renewable energy, soon planes, trains and ships will follow.

Remember nothing happens till you start to believe in the future. Thoughts create your future, so BELIEVE!!! New technology is waiting to be discovered and so much more can be yours now. My wish for all of you is to understand how powerful you truly are and how you can shape your future from thought. Your abilities are far beyond what you think. Stretch yourselves and open to all that awaits you.

MESSAGE #26
YOUR HEART

Your heart is the portal through which God sends you His love. It is also a clear lens which lets those of the higher realms see into you. It is like a window for us to see what truly fills your heart and soul.

Are you filled with compassion, tolerance and love? Or are you filled with evil, indifference and fear? You can not hide your heart's true identity from God or us. It is visible and shines open and clear, it magnifies your true soul. You may lie in words and deeds to others but not to us and definitely not to God.

You can feel when your heart is full of love and you can feel when it has been hurt. Feelings and deeds can hurt your heart more than any other organ in your body. Your heart is the center where your soul abides. It is the organ of love and is always connected to God's love. It is continuously being filled by His never ending supply of love.

When your heart is hurt it can physically hurt and ache for the loss of a dear one or a betrayal by a friend. Never underestimate the power of your heart to heal, feel, love and change as you see fit to do. No other organ is as transparent or can change as quickly as your heart.

Not only does it house most of your soul and is the portal through which God's love is passed on to you, but it also is the center where you pass love and your energies to others. With each heart beat love flows in and out of you, it beats in rhythm to the universe, pulsating love to all you direct it to. With each beat, love slips quietly into your heart and from there feeds your whole being. When you give love to another it quietly slips out and fills them up with your love and energy. This cycle never ends.

The more you give to others the more you are refilled with God's love.

Keep your heart open to be filled with God's love so that joy can overflow from within you.

MESSAGE #27 YOUR EYES AND EARS

Your eyes can deceive and show you things that are untrue. What you see is not real. What seems real to you is an elaborate hologram created by you. You created all this to act out your life in an elaborate play. All of you are characters in this drama and in each lifetime you take on a new role and act out another play.

Your ears can also deceive you. If you listen to your heart and soul and follow their path you would never be lost or deceived. Hearing and sight are wonderful gifts, but they can deform and change reality. Wouldn't it be fascinating if you could see and hear people from your heart and soul, not your eyes and ears. You would know instantly what kind of person they truly are. Skin color or looks would never play into one's consideration and different languages would never influence your perception of a person. Honesty could not be hidden, everyone would be naked with their true feelings exposed. Your discriminations of people color your judgement. You judge by sight and sound before really knowing someone. You make snap decisions on these quick assessments.

If you could only feel one's soul all preconceived judgments would be eliminated. The true self would be exposed for good or bad. How wonderful the world could be if you could see and hear from your heart, not just from your eyes or ears. Knowing you are living in a hologram and things are not real should tell you how unreliable your senses are. Open your heart to see and feel the soul of another. Only then do you get the real and honest picture of a person.

The word heart has the word "hear" in it. Your heart never lies, use it to hear the truth in others. Judge people from your heart and soul not from your tainted eyes and ears. When you know a soul from your heart, only truth will show through.

MESSAGE #28
SLEEP

A third of your life you spend in sleep yet as much as you know about sleep there is still more to understand.

In sleep, at least 3-4 times a week, your soul leaves your body to travel and reconnect with loved ones in Heaven. You don't always sleep to rest your body, you sleep to let your soul loose from the confines of the body, to be free. Your soul is almost weightless and can travel anywhere it wishes at will. While your soul is in your body it is confined to its human form, but in sleep it releases and flies free.

Dreams come in many forms and types. Bad dreams or nightmares can be your soul's way to tell or warn you about something. Symbolically the fear you feel might be a wake up call to help you pay attention to something happening in your life.

Many dreams are visitation dreams. These dreams are always in color and they are remembered in great detail. You go and visit a loved one in Heaven or they come and visit with you. They always seem very "real", that is because they are real. These dreams are not easily forgotten.

Some dreams show the future helping you to see what is to come. Dreams come in many varieties and carry many meanings. Dream meanings are as varied as the dreams themselves and only the individual may truly understand and interpret their meaning.

Sleep is needed by most entities. Trees and plants sleep in the winter, even part of Earth rests during the winter months. It is her time to reconnect with the universal rhythms and reset herself to that energy flow.

Sleep opens doorways for communication from Guides and Angels to download ideas and solutions to problems. All of a sudden you awake with a new idea or solution, you had help, you just may not remember it.

Sleep is so important for your soul to reconnect with its higher self which is in Heaven. Not all of your soul fits into your body so part of it is waiting for you in Heaven. Your soul needs this reconnection. Many nights you travel throughout the universe doing work or performing tasks that are needed of you. You may not know that you have a vocation in Heaven that requires your services while you sleep. Your body may not remember, but your soul does.

Sleep offers so much more than just rest. It opens doorways to the higher realms, visitation with loved ones, inspirations for problems, soul night work and much more.

Sleep is a necessary and integral part of your life.

I wish you all sweet dreams.

MESSAGE #29
GOOD BYE

These messages are for the world, they are for all mankind. If you can accept these messages as truths then you are on the threshold of opening up to understanding. This ascension is the next step forward for humankind. Higher beings of the universe are waiting for you to step forward and claim your rightful place. We are all applauding your progress knowing it will lead to a more peaceful world.

Your lives are changing as you yourselves are changing. Accept these with grace and know that they are for your good and growth. Be brave as you go forward. Fear leads down a dark path and dead ends you into a corner. Believe, dream, get excited for what is coming and the wonderful advances. We will happily assist you, all you have to do is ask.

In the future hunger and poverty will be wiped out, clean water and air will be achieved and yes climate change can be stopped and some of it reversed. So much can happen when you believe in your future.

God has always been at your side. His love is beyond your comprehension, but it encompasses the universe and all that are in it. His love is the power that binds us all together. It is universal magic.

Open your eyes to all the possibilities that await you and follow your heart. Use these messages as a springboard to open your soul to new ideas. Start fresh with a new outlook of positive trust. You are magnificent light filled beings and your abilities for good are boundless.

Never forget the love from which you were created. It runs through you like the DNA in your cells. Embrace all the good and strive for more and never lose sight of what you truly are. You are everlasting souls filled with God's love.

I wish you peace, grace and always love,

Gabriel